A WEEKLY JOURNAL FOR BUSY PEOPLE

.....

ESPECIALLY THOSE WITH YOUNG KIDS

Being the true record and account of wonderful and lustrous events that occured thoughout the year, this journal will be enjoyed for many years to come. When memories lapse and parents and loved ones go, this book will serve to bring back memories of those wonderful times when we were all together and life was just so....

This Journal records the memeorable events and other important details of

_____'s Life and Times

During the Year _____

This book belongs to:

_____

If found, please contact me at:

Phone: _____

Email: _____

Thanks.

Copyright © 2014 by T. Hubbard
All rights reserved.

ISBN: 978-0-9912927-3-8

New History
(a Division of ProseWorks Media)
Chapel Hill, NC

Email purchase and other inquiries to:
info@proseworks.us

"Always carry a notebook. And I mean always. The short-term memory only retains information for three minutes; unless it is committed to paper you can lose an idea for ever."
---Will Self

My journal is a storehouse, a treasury for everything in my daily life: the stories I hear, the people I meet, the quotations I like, and even the subtle signs and symbols I encounter that speak to me indirectly.
   ---Dorothy U. Seyler from *Patterns of Reflection*

"Fill your paper with the breathings of your own heart." -- William Wordsworth

HOW TO USE THIS JOURNAL TO CREATE A WONDERFUL FAMILY TREASURE

WEEKLY ENTRIES - Keep it simple!
This Journal is designed so you can successfully record highlights throughout the year. You might think you can't do this for the entire year, but almost anyone can maintain having just one 10-15 minute session each week to record activities.

So, pick a time sometime during the week - Sunday night, Saturday morning, Monday evening, whatever is convenient for you. and make your weekly entries. Keep it simple and don't make it a burden. Keep it fun.

And don't think this journal should just be for the young kids. Keep one for the teenagers and for young adults as well - one for everyone in the family. They'll appreciate it later.

WHAT TO RECORD
Periodically, review the list of prompts found on page 8. Record events and people that are important now and that will be interesting to someone reading the journal in the years ahead.

SKETCHES - Add sketches throughout the journal.

PHOTOGRAPHS
Once a month, print at least one picture of each person in the family and keep it in a folder or other safe place so that, at the end of the year, you can combine the pictures with the Journal and be assured you have a pretty good record of what went on during the year - a record that will be available in the future when memories start to pile up and you can't quite recall some of the details. (Take my word for it - those times will come.)

When you do print pictures, print multiple copies - one copy to go with each Journal you are keeping. So, if there are two kids and two parents in the family = 4 journals, then make 4 copies of any picture you print - one to accompany each journal.

Record on the back of the picture or in some other way, the date, place, and names of those pictured. Surprisingly, even a best friend's name can be forgotten 20 years down the road.

You don't need to end up with 200-300 electronic or print pictures. Better to select and print the good ones. Same for videos. Collect the best and print to a DVD once a month or so. Add to the Treasure Box.

TREASURE BOX
For each journal, keep an associated treasure box - a manila envelope, box or other container - and put pictures, newspaper clippings, magazine articles, letters, DVD of collected videos, and other mementos of the year. Make it a true treasure box. (Don't worry about ordering or organizing but do be sure to record names, places, and dates for items you save!!)

AT THE END OF THE JOURNAL YEAR
Go through the items in the Treasure Box and be sure you have annotated any item that needs names and dates. Place the journal in the Treasure Box. And know you have created a wonderful treasure for your loved one. Keep it someplace safe until you can make a wonderful gift of it.

NEXT YEAR
Learn from the experience and make the next year's journal even better. Make recording in the journal something you look forward to. Keep it simple. and make it fun. Creating this journal for someone is truly a wonderful thing you will be doing - both for your kids and for yourself.

Sample Page

Joe and Papa took Livi and Danny camping - this was the first time they had camped in the snow. It wasn't cold but it got very windy and wet.

When dawn broke, we realized that the KOA campground had been flooded by all the rain during the night, their internet service had been shut down, and we had slept in soggy sleeping bags and nothing was dry. However, at a small village market 100 meters north, we found that a bagel with cream cheese and a hot cup of coffee can do wonders. . All in all it was a great trip. And that polar bear we saw was a highlight.

Next time, we will bring a stove and better flashlights. And more s'mores.

Weather This Week

A great week - no snow

WEEK # 12
1/17 to 1/24

Visitors / Parties

Bert, Susan, Margie, little Tommy Tucker and Liza Jane, Molly and Fred all came to the birthday party.

Things That Happened

Danny birthday party was a huge success. The pinana was smacked by Livi. Dad was promoted to new job as the Boss. I got a gold star at my yoga class.

World & Local News This Week

Earthquake in N. California and volcano eruption in Papua New Guinea - Syria and the Maldives agree on Climate Change Mitigation Support Treaty. There has been no snow in the Rockies - ski areas hope to open soon. The Mayor and the Sec of Commerce announced their engagement. NC Solar installations hit record high.

Fun Stuff We Did

M
T
(W)
T
F
S
S

We wll went over to Jan and Dean's house for a cookout even though the temp was in the 30s. Steamed oysters and hotdogs for the kids - great fun. Jan's parents and their boys were back in town from Brazil.

Favorites: Activities, Friends, Music, Sports, Art, Things I am Good At

Suzie's favorite thing in all the world to do is sit wonderingly staring out the window and drawing pictures. Usually of the boy next door. Danny writes his cousin Roro trying to discover the secret code of robots.

SOME SUGGESTED TOPICS TO RECORD THROUGHOUT THE YEAR

What made this week special

Favorite Activities

Favorite Toys

Favorite Books

Favorite Movies

Favorite Song

Favorite Grandparent (just kidding)

Things I am good at

Cool things I said this week

My favorite sayings & songs

Partners and Friends

New Skills and talents

Things I am interested in

Dreams

Birthdays

Special Victories

Good Friends, Best Friends

School Activities

Art Projects

Music

Sports

Favorite Teachers and subjects in School

Teacher's names

Current News & Headlines

Grandparents and cousins

Pets

Parent Activities

Trips

Presents: given and received

Favorite Food

Cars

Things we did with favorite people

Weight and Height

Trips we took- near and far

Favorite Christmas and other presents

The Journal

Weather This Week

WEEK #_____
_____ to _____

Things That Happened

Visitors / Parties

World & Local News This Week

Fun Stuff We Did

M

T

W

T

F

S

S

Favorites: Activities, Friends, Music, Sports, Art, Things I am Good At

Weather This Week

WEEK #_____
_____ to _____

Things That Happened

Visitors / Parties

World & Local News This Week

Fun Stuff We Did

M

T

W

T

F

S

S

Favorites: Activities, Friends, Music, Sports, Art, Things I am Good At

Weather This Week

WEEK #_____
_____ to _____

Things That Happened

Visitors / Parties

World & Local News This Week

Fun Stuff We Did

M

T

W

T

F

S

S

Favorites: Activities, Friends, Music, Sports, Art, Things I am Good At

Weather This Week

WEEK #_____
_____ to _____

Things That Happened

Visitors / Parties

World & Local News This Week

Fun Stuff We Did

M

T

W

T

F

S

S

Favorites: Activities, Friends, Music, Sports, Art, Things I am Good At

Weather This Week

WEEK #_____
_____ to _____

Things That Happened

Visitors / Parties

World & Local News This Week

Fun Stuff We Did

M

T

W

T

F

S

S

Favorites: Activities, Friends, Music, Sports, Art, Things I am Good At

Weather This Week

WEEK # _____
_____ to _____

Things That Happened

Visitors / Parties

World & Local News This Week

Fun Stuff We Did

M

T

W

T

F

S

S

Favorites: Activities, Friends, Music, Sports, Art, Things I am Good At

- 21 -

Weather This Week

WEEK # _____
_____ to _____

Things That Happened

Visitors / Parties

World & Local News This Week

Fun Stuff We Did

M

T

W

T

F

S

S

Favorites: Activities, Friends, Music, Sports, Art, Things I am Good At

Weather This Week

WEEK # _____
_____ to _____

Things That Happened

Visitors / Parties

World & Local News This Week

Fun Stuff We Did

M

T

W

T

F

S

S

Favorites: Activities, Friends, Music, Sports, Art, Things I am Good At

Weather This Week

WEEK #_____
_____ to _____

Things That Happened

Visitors / Parties

Fun Stuff We Did

World & Local News This Week

M

T

W

T

F

S

S

Favorites: Activities, Friends, Music, Sports, Art, Things I am Good At

Weather This Week

WEEK #_____
_____ to _____

Things That Happened

Visitors / Parties

World & Local News This Week

Fun Stuff We Did

M

T

W

T

F

S

S

Favorites: Activities, Friends, Music, Sports, Art, Things I am Good At

Weather This Week

WEEK #_____
_____ to _____

Things That Happened

Visitors / Parties

World & Local News This Week

Fun Stuff We Did

M

T

W

T

F

S

S

Favorites: Activities, Friends, Music, Sports, Art, Things I am Good At

Weather This Week

WEEK #_____
_____ to _____

Things That Happened

Visitors / Parties

World & Local News This Week

Fun Stuff We Did

M

T

W

T

F

S

S

Favorites: Activities, Friends, Music, Sports, Art, Things I am Good At

Weather This Week

WEEK #_____
_____ to _____

Things That Happened

Visitors / Parties

World & Local News This Week

Fun Stuff We Did

M

T

W

T

F

S

S

Favorites: Activities, Friends, Music, Sports, Art, Things I am Good At

Weather This Week

WEEK # _____
_____ to _____

Visitors / Parties

Things That Happened

Fun Stuff We Did

World & Local News This Week

M

T

W

T

F

S

S

Favorites: Activities, Friends, Music, Sports, Art, Things I am Good At

Weather This Week

WEEK #_____
_____ to _____

Things That Happened

Visitors / Parties

World & Local News This Week

Fun Stuff We Did

M

T

W

T

F

S

S

Favorites: Activities, Friends, Music, Sports, Art, Things I am Good At

Weather This Week

WEEK # _____
_____ to _____

Things That Happened

Visitors / Parties

World & Local News This Week

Fun Stuff We Did

M

T

W

T

F

S

S

Favorites: Activities, Friends, Music, Sports, Art, Things I am Good At

Weather This Week

WEEK #_____
_____ to _____

Things That Happened

Visitors / Parties

World & Local News This Week

Fun Stuff We Did

M

T

W

T

F

S

S

Favorites: Activities, Friends, Music, Sports, Art, Things I am Good At

Weather This Week

WEEK # _____
_____ to _____

Visitors / Parties

Things That Happened

World & Local News This Week

Fun Stuff We Did

M

T

W

T

F

S

S

Favorites: Activities, Friends, Music, Sports, Art, Things I am Good At

Weather This Week

WEEK # _____
_____ to _____

Things That Happened

Visitors / Parties

World & Local News This Week

Fun Stuff We Did

M

T

W

T

F

S

S

Favorites: Activities, Friends, Music, Sports, Art, Things I am Good At

Weather This Week

WEEK #_____
_____ to _____

Things That Happened

Visitors / Parties

World & Local News This Week

Fun Stuff We Did

M

T

W

T

F

S

S

Favorites: Activities, Friends, Music, Sports, Art, Things I am Good At

Weather This Week

WEEK #_____
_____ to _____

Things That Happened

Visitors / Parties

World & Local News This Week

Fun Stuff We Did

M

T

W

T

F

S

S

Favorites: Activities, Friends, Music, Sports, Art, Things I am Good At

Weather This Week

WEEK # _____
_____ to _____

Things That Happened

Visitors / Parties

World & Local News This Week

Fun Stuff We Did

M

T

W

T

F

S

S

Favorites: Activities, Friends, Music, Sports, Art, Things I am Good At

Weather This Week

WEEK #_____
_____ to _____

Things That Happened

Visitors / Parties

World & Local News This Week

Fun Stuff We Did

M

T

W

T

F

S

S

Favorites: Activities, Friends, Music, Sports, Art, Things I am Good At

Weather This Week

WEEK #_____
_____ to _____

Things That Happened

Visitors / Parties

World & Local News This Week

Fun Stuff We Did

M

T

W

T

F

S

S

Favorites: Activities, Friends, Music, Sports, Art, Things I am Good At

Weather This Week

WEEK #_____
_____ to _____

Things That Happened

Visitors / Parties

World & Local News This Week

Fun Stuff We Did

M

T

W

T

F

S

S

Favorites: Activities, Friends, Music, Sports, Art, Things I am Good At

Weather This Week

WEEK #_____
_____ to _____

Things That Happened

Visitors / Parties

World & Local News This Week

Fun Stuff We Did

M

T

W

T

F

S

S

Favorites: Activities, Friends, Music, Sports, Art, Things I am Good At

Weather This Week

WEEK #_____
_____ to _____

Things That Happened

Visitors / Parties

Fun Stuff We Did

World & Local News This Week

M

T

W

T

F

S

S

Favorites: Activities, Friends, Music, Sports, Art, Things I am Good At

Weather This Week

WEEK # _____
_____ to _____

Things That Happened

Visitors / Parties

World & Local News This Week

Fun Stuff We Did

M

T

W

T

F

S

S

Favorites: Activities, Friends, Music, Sports, Art, Things I am Good At

Weather This Week

WEEK #_____
_____ to _____

Things That Happened

Visitors / Parties

World & Local News This Week

Fun Stuff We Did

M

T

W

T

F

S

S

Favorites: Activities, Friends, Music, Sports, Art, Things I am Good At

Weather This Week

WEEK # _____
_____ to _____

Things That Happened

Visitors / Parties

World & Local News This Week

Fun Stuff We Did

M

T

W

T

F

S

S

Favorites: Activities, Friends, Music, Sports, Art, Things I am Good At

Weather This Week

WEEK # _____
_____ to _____

Things That Happened

Visitors / Parties

World & Local News This Week

Fun Stuff We Did

M

T

W

T

F

S

S

Favorites: Activities, Friends, Music, Sports, Art, Things I am Good At

Weather This Week

WEEK #_____
_____ to _____

Things That Happened

Visitors / Parties

World & Local News This Week

Fun Stuff We Did

M

T

W

T

F

S

S

Favorites: Activities, Friends, Music, Sports, Art, Things I am Good At

Weather This Week

WEEK #_____
_____ to _____

Things That Happened

Visitors / Parties

World & Local News This Week

Fun Stuff We Did

M

T

W

T

F

S

S

Favorites: Activities, Friends, Music, Sports, Art, Things I am Good At

Weather This Week

WEEK #_____
_____ to _____

Things That Happened

Visitors / Parties

World & Local News This Week

Fun Stuff We Did

M

T

W

T

F

S

S

Favorites: Activities, Friends, Music, Sports, Art, Things I am Good At

Weather This Week

WEEK #_____
_____ to _____

Things That Happened

Visitors / Parties

World & Local News This Week

Fun Stuff We Did

M

T

W

T

F

S

S

Favorites: Activities, Friends, Music, Sports, Art, Things I am Good At

Weather This Week

WEEK #_____
_____ to _____

Things That Happened

Visitors / Parties

World & Local News This Week

Fun Stuff We Did

M

T

W

T

F

S

S

Favorites: Activities, Friends, Music, Sports, Art, Things I am Good At

Weather This Week

WEEK #_____
_____ to _____

Things That Happened

Visitors / Parties

World & Local News This Week

Fun Stuff We Did

M

T

W

T

F

S

S

Favorites: Activities, Friends, Music, Sports, Art, Things I am Good At

Weather This Week

WEEK #_____
_____ to _____

Things That Happened

Visitors / Parties

World & Local News This Week

Fun Stuff We Did

M

T

W

T

F

S

S

Favorites: Activities, Friends, Music, Sports, Art, Things I am Good At

Weather This Week

WEEK #_____
_____ to _____

Things That Happened

Visitors / Parties

World & Local News This Week

Fun Stuff We Did

M

T

W

T

F

S

S

Favorites: Activities, Friends, Music, Sports, Art, Things I am Good At

Weather This Week

WEEK #_____
_____ to _____

Things That Happened

Visitors / Parties

World & Local News This Week

Fun Stuff We Did

M

T

W

T

F

S

S

Favorites: Activities, Friends, Music, Sports, Art, Things I am Good At

Weather This Week

WEEK #_____
_____ to _____

Things That Happened

Visitors / Parties

World & Local News This Week

Fun Stuff We Did

M

T

W

T

F

S

S

Favorites: Activities, Friends, Music, Sports, Art, Things I am Good At

Weather This Week

WEEK # _____
_____ to _____

Things That Happened

Visitors / Parties

World & Local News This Week

Fun Stuff We Did

M

T

W

T

F

S

S

Favorites: Activities, Friends, Music, Sports, Art, Things I am Good At

Weather This Week

WEEK # _____
_____ to _____

Things That Happened

Visitors / Parties

World & Local News This Week

Fun Stuff We Did

M

T

W

T

F

S

S

Favorites: Activities, Friends, Music, Sports, Art, Things I am Good At

Weather This Week

WEEK # _____
_____ to _____

Things That Happened

Visitors / Parties

World & Local News This Week

Fun Stuff We Did

M

T

W

T

F

S

S

Favorites: Activities, Friends, Music, Sports, Art, Things I am Good At

Weather This Week

WEEK #_____
_____ to _____

Things That Happened

Visitors / Parties

World & Local News This Week

Fun Stuff We Did

M

T

W

T

F

S

S

Favorites: Activities, Friends, Music, Sports, Art, Things I am Good At

Weather This Week

WEEK #_____
_____ to _____

Things That Happened

Visitors / Parties

World & Local News This Week

Fun Stuff We Did

M

T

W

T

F

S

S

Favorites: Activities, Friends, Music, Sports, Art, Things I am Good At

Weather This Week

WEEK #_____
_____ to _____

Things That Happened

Visitors / Parties

World & Local News This Week

Fun Stuff We Did

M

T

W

T

F

S

S

Favorites: Activities, Friends, Music, Sports, Art, Things I am Good At

Weather This Week

WEEK #_____
_____ to _____

Things That Happened

Visitors / Parties

World & Local News This Week

Fun Stuff We Did

M

T

W

T

F

S

S

Favorites: Activities, Friends, Music, Sports, Art, Things I am Good At

Weather This Week

WEEK #_____
_____ to _____

Things That Happened

Visitors / Parties

World & Local News This Week

Fun Stuff We Did

M

T

W

T

F

S

S

Favorites: Activities, Friends, Music, Sports, Art, Things I am Good At

Weather This Week

WEEK #_____
_____ to _____

Things That Happened

Visitors / Parties

World & Local News This Week

Fun Stuff We Did

M

T

W

T

F

S

S

Favorites: Activities, Friends, Music, Sports, Art, Things I am Good At

Weather This Week

WEEK #_____
_____ to _____

Things That Happened

Visitors / Parties

World & Local News This Week

Fun Stuff We Did

M

T

W

T

F

S

S

Favorites: Activities, Friends, Music, Sports, Art, Things I am Good At

Weather This Week

WEEK #_____
_____ to _____

Things That Happened

Visitors / Parties

World & Local News This Week

Fun Stuff We Did

M

T

W

T

F

S

S

Favorites: Activities, Friends, Music, Sports, Art, Things I am Good At

Weather This Week

WEEK #_____
_____ to _____

Things That Happened

Visitors / Parties

World & Local News This Week

Fun Stuff We Did

M

T

W

T

F

S

S

Favorites: Activities, Friends, Music, Sports, Art, Things I am Good At

Weather This Week

WEEK #_____
_____ to _____

Things That Happened

Visitors / Parties

World & Local News This Week

Fun Stuff We Did

M

T

W

T

F

S

S

Favorites: Activities, Friends, Music, Sports, Art, Things I am Good At

Weather This Week

WEEK # _____
_____ to _____

Things That Happened

Visitors / Parties

World & Local News This Week

Fun Stuff We Did

M

T

W

T

F

S

S

Favorites: Activities, Friends, Music, Sports, Art, Things I am Good At

Weather This Week

WEEK #_____
_____ to _____

Things That Happened

Visitors / Parties

World & Local News This Week

Fun Stuff We Did

M

T

W

T

F

S

S

Favorites: Activities, Friends, Music, Sports, Art, Things I am Good At

Weather This Week

WEEK #_____
_____ to _____

Visitors / Parties

Things That Happened

Fun Stuff We Did

World & Local News This Week

M

T

W

T

F

S

S

Favorites: Activities, Friends, Music, Sports, Art, Things I am Good At

Weather This Week

WEEK #_____
_____ to _____

Things That Happened

Visitors / Parties

World & Local News This Week

Fun Stuff We Did

M

T

W

T

F

S

S

Favorites: Activities, Friends, Music, Sports, Art, Things I am Good At

Weather This Week

WEEK #_____
_____ to _____

Things That Happened

Visitors / Parties

World & Local News This Week

Fun Stuff We Did

M

T

W

T

F

S

S

Favorites: Activities, Friends, Music, Sports, Art, Things I am Good At

Weather This Week

WEEK #_____
_____ to _____

Things That Happened

Visitors / Parties

World & Local News This Week

Fun Stuff We Did

M

T

W

T

F

S

S

Favorites: Activities, Friends, Music, Sports, Art, Things I am Good At

Weather This Week

WEEK # _____
_____ to _____

Things That Happened

Visitors / Parties

World & Local News This Week

Fun Stuff We Did

M

T

W

T

F

S

S

Favorites: Activities, Friends, Music, Sports, Art, Things I am Good At

www.ingramcontent.com/pod-product-compliance
Lightning Source LLC
Chambersburg PA
CBHW051755040426
42446CB00007B/371